THE HOOKMAN

This series features unsolved mysteries, urban legends, and other curious stories. Each creepy, shocking, or befuddling book focuses on what people believe and hear. True or not? That's for you to decide!

 45th Parallel Press

Published in the United States of America by Cherry Lake Publishing
Ann Arbor, Michigan
www.cherrylakepublishing.com

Reading Adviser: Marla Conn MS, Ed., Literacy specialist, Read-Ability, Inc.
Book Designer: Felicia Macheske

Photo Credits: © Mikhail Klyoshev/Shutterstock.com, cover; © grafxart/Shutterstock.com, 5; © Fotovika/
Shutterstock.com, 7; © SpeedKingz/Shutterstock.com, 8; © Bruno Passigatti/Shutterstock.com, 11; © Kamira/
Shutterstock.com, 12; © Arman Zhenikeyev/Shutterstock.com, 15; © Alexander Y/Shutterstock.com, 17;©
gpointstudio/Shutterstock.com, 18; © Prath/Shutterstock.com, 20; © KucherAV/Shutterstock.com, 23; ©
Photographee.eu/Shutterstock.com, 24; © CREATISTA/Shutterstock.com, 27; © Ivan Roth/Shutterstock.com, 29

Graphic Elements Throughout: © iofoto/Shutterstock.com; © COLCU/Shutterstock.com; © spacedrone808/
Shutterstock.com; © rf.vector.stock/Shutterstock.com; © donatas1205/Shutterstock.com; © cluckva/
Shutterstock.com; © Eky Studio/Shutterstock.com

45th Parallel Press is an imprint of Cherry Lake Publishing.

Library of Congress Cataloging-in-Publication Data has been filed and is available at catalog.loc.gov

Cherry Lake Publishing would like to acknowledge the work of The Partnership for 21st Century Skills.
Please visit *www.p21.org* for more information.

Printed in the United States of America
Corporate Graphics

TABLE OF CONTENTS

Chapter One
HOOKING A GOOD STORY...................4

Chapter Two
BEWARE THE HANGING HOOK........10

Chapter Three
FROM PHANTOM TO HOOKMAN.......16

Chapter Four
YOU'VE BEEN WARNED!................22

Chapter Five
IT'S ALL IN THE TELLING!............26

DID YOU KNOW?..........................30
CONSIDER THIS!...........................31
LEARN MORE..............................31
GLOSSARY...............................32
INDEX...................................32
ABOUT THE AUTHOR.....................32

Chapter One

HOOKING A GOOD STORY

What are different versions of the Hookman story? How do the stories affect people?

There are many stories about the Hookman. This is one story. A woman goes to a gas station. She gets gas. She pays. Her credit card doesn't work. The cashier makes a phone call. He asks her to go to his office. She says no. He grabs her. He pushes her to the ground. He pulls out a gun. She screams.

The gun isn't aimed at her. The cashier goes to her car. He points the gun at Hookman. Hookman had crept into her car. He was in the backseat. The cashier shoots Hookman. The cops show up. The cashier had called them. He saw Hookman coming. The woman now always checks her backseat.

Hookman can show up in different places.

CONSIDER THE EVIDENCE

Having a hook for a hand is real. It allows amputees to have some control. Amputees are people who lose limbs. At first, people used regular hooks. These hooks were made of iron or wood. They were heavy. They were clumsy. Ambroise Pare created better hooks. He was a surgeon. He lived in the 1500s. He worked on battlefields. His hooks were wood covered with metal. D.W. Dorrance lost his arm. He had an accident at work. He made his own hook. He invented a split hook design. He did this in 1912. His hook worked better. It let amputees do more things.

This is another story about Hookman. A group of girls go camping. (Some say the girls are Girl Scouts.) The adult tells everyone to stay together. But one girl doesn't listen. She walks away from camp. Hookman sees her. He kills her with his hook. He leaves his hook behind. The other campers look for the girl. They find the hook instead.

This story scares campers. Adults tell it to make campers stay together. They want to keep campers safe. They don't want campers to wander off.

Hookman is a good story to tell around a bonfire.

Hookman is a stalker. This means he follows people.

This is another story about Hookman. Hookman is a **serial** killer. Serial means repeating. Serial killers kill many people. They have a type of **victim**. Victims are targets of crimes. Serial killers kill victims in the same way.

Hookman targets women. He follows them. He figures out their cars. He hides under their cars. He waits. Women walk to their cars. Hookman slices their ankles. He uses his hook. He pulls them under the car.

This story scares women. Women protect themselves. They check under their cars. They look for Hookman.

Chapter Two

BEWARE THE HANGING HOOK

Who is the Hookman? What is the common Hookman story?

Hookman is a killer. He doesn't have a hand. No one knows how he lost his hand. He has a hook instead. His hook is sharp. It has a pointy tip. It's made of stainless steel. No one knows what he looks like. Some stories say he wears a long coat. The focus is his hook.

Hookman escaped. Some stories say he escaped from prison. This makes him a criminal. Some stories say he escaped from a mental hospital. This makes him crazy. No one knows his history.

Hookman is mysterious. No one knows where he came from.

The Hookman story convinces kids not to lie to parents.

There's one common story about Hookman. Two teens start dating. They lie to their parents. They say they're going to the movies. But instead, they go to Lovers' Lane. This is where teens go to kiss.

They listen to the radio. There's a special news report. The radio announcer states a warning. He says a serial killer escaped. He says the killer has a hook.

They hear a sound. It's a scraping sound. It's on the car. The girl gets scared. She wants to go home. The boy doesn't want to go yet. He tells her not to worry.

BIOGRAPHY

Captain Kristin Nelson is a 23rd Bomb Squadron pilot. She got a new house. She was using a saw to do repairs on the house. She had an accident. She lost her left hand. She said, "It was crazy how it all happened." She stayed calm. She saved her hand. She put it on ice. But she was worried about her job. How can pilots fly without a hand? She said, "I started flying when I was 14 years old. It's part of who I am." A doctor put her hand back on. This operation rarely works. A doctor reattached the bones, veins, and muscles. She was able to fly 11 months later.

The boy blames the branches for the sound. Tree branches blow in the wind. They scrape the car. The girl believes him. But they keep hearing scraping sounds. The girl wants to go home again. She insists. The boy listens to her. They leave in a hurry. They speed off.

The boy takes the girl home. They're in her driveway. They get out of the car. They look at the door handle. They scream. They see a hook. The hook is hanging on the handle. The hook is bloody. It was ripped from a body.

In some stories, Hookman kills the teens.

Chapter Three

FROM PHANTOM TO HOOKMAN

What is the history of the Hookman story?
What are the Lovers' Lane murders?

Hookman is one of the most famous **urban legends**. Urban legends are modern folktales. This story traces back to the 1950s. This makes sense. Cars were popular at this time. More people owned them. More people were driving. Cars gave teens more freedom. Parents worried about them.

The Hookman story was first printed in 1960. The exact date was November 8, 1960. It was printed in a "Dear Abby" column. People wrote to Abby. They shared their problems. They asked for advice. Someone wrote, "If you are interested in teenagers, you will print this story." The person told the story of Hookman.

Hookman was one of the first urban legends.

Every newspaper and radio reported the story.

Hookman is based on real murders. It's based on the Lovers' Lane murders. It's also called the Texarkana Moonlight Murders. Texarkana is a city. It's between Texas and Arkansas.

The murders happened in 1946. They happened during the late winter and early spring. They happened over 10 weeks. They happened during the weekends. Eight people were attacked. Five of them died. The killer was called "the **Phantom** Killer." Phantom means a ghost. The killer was never caught. No one knows who the killer is.

CONNECTION

Roy Alexander doesn't like hooks. He's from England. He strapped furniture to his car. He used a bungee cord. The bungee cord snapped into his face. A metal hook stuck in his left eye. It hooked around the back of his eye. He screamed. His wife's name is Judith. She ran outside. She saw a cord dangling from his eye. The other end was still stuck to the car. His wife cut the cord. She rushed him to the hospital. Alexander held the hook in place. He did this for 3 hours. Doctors removed the hook. Alexander didn't feel anything. He was in shock.

The FBI and Texas Rangers investigated the Texarkana Moonlight Murders.

The killer attacked late at night. He went to Lovers' Lanes. He used a gun. He attacked couples. He shot them. Their bodies were found the next morning.

The town was scared. They panicked. They armed themselves. They bought guard dogs. They locked themselves inside. They covered windows. They booby-trapped their homes. They left lights on. Some people left town. Cops walked the neighborhoods. They walked the streets. They looked for any signs of the killer.

The case remains unsolved. This led to stories. This led to Hookman.

Chapter Four

YOU'VE BEEN WARNED!

What did Bengt af Klintberg think? What did Bill Ellis think? What are other thoughts about Hookman?

Bengt af Klintberg is a folklorist. He studies urban legends. He's Swedish. He's highly respected. The Swedish word for urban legends is *klintbergare*.

Klintberg studies Hookman. He said it's an example of **conflict**. Conflict means fighting. People are torn between good and evil. Some people follow rules. Some people don't follow rules. Rule breakers are **deviants**. This means they're not normal. They threaten the normal group.

Hookman scares people. The story tells people to follow rules. It tells them not to do bad things. It's a **cautionary** tale. This means it's a warning.

Klintberg works with communities to collect stories.

Bill Ellis is a folklorist. He's from the United States. He thinks Hookman is a "**moral custodian**." Moral means good behavior. Custodian means a guard. Hookman punishes teens for breaking rules. He punishes them for lying.

Some folklorists think the radio in the Hookman story is important. The radio is the "voice of **conscience**." Conscience is an inner voice. It tells right from wrong. It warned the teens. In the story, the girl wanted to leave. She was doing the right thing. If she hadn't, they would've died. The Hookman story has a lesson. It tells teens to be good.

The teens had a close call.

INVESTIGATION TIPS

- Get the local newspaper. Read the crime reports. Keep track of prison escapes. Keep track of mental hospital escapes.

- Go to the library. Read different versions of the Hookman.

- Sign up for overnight camps. Go to campfire events. Listen to the stories. Watch how people react.

- Talk to people who tell the Hookman story. Ask them where they first heard the story. Ask them how they feel about the story.

- Talk to folklorists. Ask them about urban legends.

- Join the American Folklore Society. This is a group. Members study stories. They collect community stories. They write books. They make movies. They host events.

Chapter Five

IT'S ALL IN THE TELLING!

How and why does this story change?
How is this story scary?

People spread Hookman stories. They've been doing this for a long time. They tell it all over the United States. The stories are pretty similar. The place changes. Hookman is from wherever the storyteller is. The story is scarier if people think Hookman is close by.

Adults mostly tell it. They tell the story to teens. They want teens to be safe. The story is told **orally**. Orally means it's not written down. This means people can add their own spins.

The story is mostly told at night. It's popular at camps. It's popular at **sleepovers**. Sleepovers are when friends spend the night.

Adults want teens to make good choices.

EXPLAINED BY SCIENCE

The Hookman could be a psychopath. Psychopathy is a personality disorder. Psychopaths don't feel guilt. They don't care about other people's feelings. They aren't social. They prefer to be alone. They do whatever they want. They're selfish. Some psychopaths commit violent crimes. They hurt other people. They use other people. They're not psychotic. Psychotic means crazy. Psychotic people don't have control of their minds. They may see things. They may hear voices. But psychopaths are different. They know exactly what they're doing. They're in control. They choose to do bad things. The FBI states that serial killers tend to be psychopathic.

Storytellers can make the story more interesting. They add details. They add sound effects. They use a hook as a prop. They speak in a scary voice.

Hookman is scary. He's not real. But he could be. This is what makes Hookman scary. The story is crazy. But it's in a real setting. It involves real people. It involves real things. It could happen. But no one can be sure. It's still unbelievable. It picks at human fears. It tricks people. It makes them think their fears are real.

Real or not? It doesn't matter. Hookman lives in people's imaginations.

Urban legends are sometimes also called everyday tales.

DID YOU KNOW?

- Captain James Hook is from *Peter Pan*. *Peter Pan* is a story by J. M. Barrie. Captain Hook has a hook for a hand. He's a pirate captain. His ship is called the *Jolly Roger*. Peter Pan cut off his hand. Then, a crocodile ate the hand. Captain Hook replaced his hand with an iron hook. He's the most famous man with a hook.

- Luke Skywalker is from *Star Wars*. He's a famous character. He lost his right hand. This happened in a battle.

- Claus von Stauffenberg was a real person. He was a German army officer. He's famous for trying to get rid of Hitler. He was in a battle in Tunisia. This was in 1943. Stauffenberg was badly injured. He lost an eye. He lost his right hand. He lost two fingers on his left hand.

- *Supernatural* is a popular TV show. It has an episode based on the Hookman. This episode aired in 2005.

- *I Know What You Did Last Summer* is a 1997 movie. The killer uses a hook. The main characters tell the story of the Hookman.

CONSIDER THIS!

Take a Position: Some people think the Hookman story is too scary to tell. Argue your point with reasons and evidence.

Say What? Reread Chapter Four. What do you think Hookman is about? Explain the lesson that is being taught. Explain how the story affects your behavior.

Think About It! Why are there so many different versions of this story? How would you change the story? Why would you make these changes?

LEARN MORE

- Schwartz, Alvin. *Scary Stories to Tell in the Dark*. New York: HarperCollins Publishers, 2005.
- Young, Richard, and Judy Dockrey Young. *Favorite Scary Stories of American Children*. Little Rock, AR: August House, 1999.

GLOSSARY

cautionary (KAW-shuhn-ayr-ee) warning

conflict (KAHN-flikt) fight

conscience (KAHN-shuhns) inner voice that tells right from wrong

custodian (kuhs-TOH-dee-uhn) a guard

deviants (DEE-vee-uhnts) people who are not normal

moral (MOR-uhl) having good behavior

orally (OR-uhl-ee) verbally, not written down

phantom (FAN-tuhm) ghost

serial (SEER-ee-uhl) repeating the same thing; of a series

sleepovers (SLEEP-oh-vurz) slumber parties; events where friends sleep over

urban legends (UR-buhn LEJ-uhndz) modern folktales

victim (VIK-tuhm) the target of a crime

INDEX

backseat, 4–5
Bengt af Klintberg, 22–23
campers, 7
cautionary tale, 23
conflict, 22
conscience, 24
Ellis, Bill, 24
hands, 6, 10, 14
hook
    caught in eye, 19
    hands, 6, 10, 15, 30

Hookman
    history of, 16–21
    stories about, 4–5, 7–9, 13, 15, 26–29, 30
    studies about, 22–24
    who he is, 10–15
Lovers' Lane, 13, 15, 18–21
murders, 18–21
Phantom Killer, 18
psychopathy, 28
radio, 13, 24

science, 28
scraping sounds, 13, 15
serial killer, 9, 13
sleepovers, 27
storytelling, 26–27, 29
teens, 13, 15, 16-17, 24, 26
Texarkana Moonlight Murders, 18–21
urban legends, 16, 22, 29
women, 9

ABOUT THE AUTHOR

Dr. Virginia Loh-Hagan is an author, university professor, former classroom teacher, and curriculum designer. She remembers hearing this story at summer camp. She was scared. She lives in San Diego with her very tall husband and very naughty dogs. To learn more about her, visit www.virginialoh.com.